Her children rise up and call her blessed; her husband also,
and he praises her: "Many daughters have done well,
but you excel them all."

PROVERBS 31:28–29 NKJV

Presented To:

Presented By:

Date:

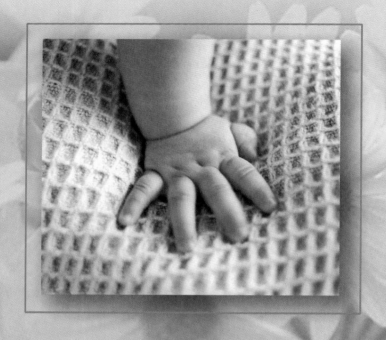

A mother holds her children's hands for a
while, but she holds their hearts forever.

AUTHOR UNKNOWN

thank you mom

BLUE SKY INK

Brentwood, Tennessee

Blessed
are the mothers
of the earth.
They combine
the practical and
the spiritual into
the workable ways
of human life.

WILLIAM L. STINGER

All your children shall be taught by
the LORD, and great shall be the peace
of your children.

ISAIAH 54:13 NKJV

For the three magic gifts
I needed to escape the poverty of my hometown,
I thank my mother, who gave me
a sewing machine, a typewriter, and a suitcase.

ALICE WALKER

gift of love

God, it seems you've been our home forever;
long before the mountains were born,
long before you brought earth itself to birth,
from "once upon a time" to
"kingdom come"—you are God.

PSALM 90:1–2 THE MESSAGE

$\mathcal{A}$ mother's arms are made of
tenderness, and children sleep
soundly in them.

VICTOR HUGO

I love you

Dear Mom,

Please know
that my little heart,
which from yours got its start,
did not from your love depart.

And when you held my little hand,
it was so wonderful and grand
and a beautiful part of God's plan.

And when you kissed my little face,
whatever time, whatever place,
you showed me God's wondrous grace.

Way to go, Mom!

Some are *kissing* mothers and some are
scolding mothers, but it is *love* just the same,
and most mothers kiss and scold together.

PEARL S. BUCK

You are He who brought me forth from the womb;
You made me trust when upon my mother's breasts.

PSALM 22:9 NASB

$\mathcal{I}$ have relied on you all my life; you have protected me since the day I was born. I will always praise you.

PSALM 71:6 GNT

A mother's love endures through all;
in good repute, in bad repute, in the face of the
world's condemnation, a mother still loves on.

WASHINGTON IRVING

mommy

Listen, my son, to your father's instruction

and do not forsake your mother's teaching.

PROVERBS 1:8 NIV

There is no *velvet* so soft as a mother's lap,

no *rose* as lovely as her smile,

no *path* so flowery as that imprinted

with her footsteps.

ARCHIBALD THOMPSON

celebrate

A mother understands what a child does not say.

YIDDISH PROVERB

We cried as we went out to plant our seeds. Now
let us celebrate as we bring in the crops. We cried
on the way to plant our seeds, but we will celebrate
and shout as we bring in the crops.

PSALM 126:5–6 CEV

Thank you, Mom,

for loving me no matter what,
for seeking me no matter where,
for defending me no matter who.

Thank you, Mom,
for wanting me to do my best,
for wanting me to have the best,
for wanting me to know what's best.

Thank you, Mom,
for knowing who you are,
for knowing who I am,
for knowing who God is.

I love you

The rainbow shall be in the cloud,
and I will look on it to remember the everlasting
covenant between God and every living creature of
all flesh that is on the earth.

GENESIS 9:16 NKJV

There is nothing sweeter than the heart of a pious mother.

MARTIN LUTHER

Blessed be the God and Father of our Lord Jesus Christ, the Father of mercies and God of all comfort, who comforts us in all our affliction so that we will be able to comfort those who are in any affliction with the comfort with which we ourselves are comforted by God.

2 CORINTHIANS 1:3–4 NASB

My mother used to look out the window every morning and say, "Maybe this will be the day when Christ comes again." She lived with that daily anticipation. It was my mother's hope until she went at last to be with him.

BILLY GRAHAM

I love you

Youth fades; love droops; the leaves of friendship fall;
a *mother's* secret hope outlives them all.

OLIVER WENDELL HOLMES

Light, space, zest—that's GOD!
So, with him on my side
I'm fearless, afraid of no one and nothing.

PSALM 27:1 THE MESSAGE

Love is not blind;

love sees a great deal more than the actual.

Love sees the ideas, the potential in us.

OSWALD CHAMBERS

There was never a *woman* like her. She was as gentle as a dove and as brave as a lioness. The memory of my mother and her teachings were, after all, the only capital I had to start life with, and on that capital I have made my way.

ANDREW JACKSON

Be strong and courageous! Do not be afraid or discouraged. For the LORD your God is with you wherever you go.

JOSHUA 1:9 NLT

Mom, you are dear to me,
for in you I see
who I am and yet can be.

From you I came;
you gave me your name;
you accept me forever the same.

In you I know of love
that comes from above
on the wings of a snow white dove.

You show me in every place
the picture of God's face,
the power of God's grace.

Thank you, dear Mom.

my mom

In all my efforts to learn to read, my
mother shared fully my ambition and
sympathized with me and aided me in every
way she could. If I have done anything in
my life worth attention, I feel sure that I
inherited the disposition from my mother.

BOOKER T. WASHINGTON

My grace is sufficient for you, for My strength
is made perfect in weakness.

2 CORINTHIANS 12:9 NKJV

Be strong and courageous, do not fear

or be dismayed . . . for the one with us is greater

than the one with him.

2 CHRONICLES 32:7 NASB

thank you, Mom

Mother love is the fuel that enables a normal human being to do the impossible.

AUTHOR UNKNOWN

GOD is all mercy and grace—not quick to anger, is rich in love. GOD is good to one and all; everything he does is suffused with grace.

PSALM 145:8–9 THE MESSAGE

Momma was home.
She was the most totally human,
human being that I have ever known;
and so very beautiful.

LEONTYNE PRICE

God gives us friends, and that means much; but far
above all others, the greatest of his gifts to earth was
when he thought of mothers.

Author Unknown

All I am I owe to my *mother*. I attribute all my success in life to the moral, intellectual, and physical education I received from her.

GEORGE WASHINGTON

I am sure that God, who began the good work within you, will continue his work until it is finally finished on that day when Christ Jesus comes back again.

PHILIPPIANS 1:6 NLT

Moms can see all over town,
up and down and around,
knowing what their children do,
praying for them through and through.

Moms know before it is done;
no thing escapes them, not one;
they suspect, sense, and feel;
they always know what is real.

And it is a mom's heart
that offers a new start,
and with a gracious nod,
brings close the love of God.

Moms are great!

I love you

Thank You, Mom
ISBN 1-59475-009-2

Copyright © 2005 by GRQ, Inc.

Published by Blue Sky Ink
Brentwood, Tennessee 37027

Editor: Lila Empson
Compiler: P. Barnhart
Design: Diane Whisner, Tulsa, Oklahoma

Printed in China.